MW00634951

Food For The Soul

From Ama's Kitchen
Soulful Vegan And Raw Vegan Recipes

Ama T. Opare

46 Easy Gourmet Recipes Even Your Non-Vegan Friends And Family Will Eat

Copyright © 2014 Ama Thandiwe Opare (Laura W. Opare) BS, MA, MA

All rights reserved.

No part of this publication may be reproduced, stored in retrieval system, copied in any form or by any means, electronic, mechanical, photocopying, recording or otherwise transmitted without prior written permission from Ama Opare and Opare Publishing, LLC.

First Edition

ISBN # 978-0-9850654-4-7

Opare Publishing, LLC

Atlanta, GA 30331, USA

www.opare.net

Cover, photographs, and book design by Ama T. Opare.

Table Of Contents

Foreword

With this book Ama has finally fulfilled the requests of our students at Opare Institute and many others who follow Ama online at Food For The Soul and on Facebook and puts in one place what heretofore you had to gather from several sites. As an added bonus she has added links to over thirty minutes of video included that are otherwise unlisted on YouTube.

Food For The Soul is an easy to access guide to the delicious, easy to make dishes Ama demonstrates and serves each session of our flagship Conscious Vegan course. What you see here is what we eat at home. The photos taken by Ama herself are those of dishes that were eaten immediately afterwards and I can attest personally were fabu-licious. Your dishes will look and, with very little practice will taste like these. They are what Ama has come to rely upon for our daily nutrition. I am truly blessed to be the second best cook in the house and know despite my long interest in cooking and healing with food I am no peer as a chef to Ama and am blessed to have my complement in the kitchen.

Having been professionally trained in food nutrition and dietetics I, have for more than three decades, have had an appreciation for creative and freshly prepared foods. I lived in San Francisco for many years where outstanding food is to be found in the over seven thousand restaurants in the 49 square miles of town. Ama has pulled many recipes from many sources and put her spin on them creating a savory and scrumptious repertoire we experience every day at home. This is the food we eat. The best restaurant I eat in is at home. Build upon these recipes and the same will be true for you. This food crosses many genres from Asian to Afrikan but as common threads are fresh, whole, organic and well seasoned. These attributes, any chef worth their knife knows, are the keys to satisfying meals.

Balancing the five basic flavors within a meal and/or even within a dish is a key to a satisfying meal. The human palate is satisfied by a combination of five basic flavors; sweet, salty, sour, bitter, spicy/savory, if artfully combined are sure to please. Most of the dishes herein are balanced within themselves. However I recommend that if you keep in mind that if you include each of the five flavors within a meal you will make your family happy and satisfied.

Ama has long been an excellent cook. She has always valued home cooked meals and has long been the person in her family who got calls on how to make this or that. She has an understanding of the use of spice, which as you will see is wonderfully and artfully expressed here. The last seven years she has devoted to becoming a world-class vegan and raw vegan cook. Food is her passion and teaching others what she knows is how she expresses it. This has been a labor of love for her that you will experience in the dishes herein. Ama is not only a great chef but is also a great photographer and videographer. She did everything in this book herself.

This is a cookbook for Black folks and those who like their foods fully flavored. You will find these recipes to be without exception well suited to the Afrikan American palate.

For those readers who are familiar with the Opare Institute, it goes without saying that all of the dishes are vegan and all except a few are raw. We teach at Opare Institute the simple fact that only whole, plant based foods are safe to eat and are the foundation of good health. Going from vegan to raw takes your food from the level of supporting good health to restoring and enhancing it. Eating a high percentage of your food raw and uncooked is a key to longevity and living without chronic disease. Living foods have amazing healing properties and if consumed while also following the rest of your Rule Book And User Guide To Healthy Living will assure you of good health throughout your life.

Although all of these recipes are vegan some are not ideally suited for an aggressive healing pattern of food consumption for those with serious or chronic illness. If you are basically well however they will sustain your health. Ama in some of the recipes found here uses oils, salts, sweeteners, vinegars and an occasional flavoring that should be avoided if you are in a remedial phase of changing the way you eat from that of a SAD diet (standard American diet.) Reversing serious disease usually requires a detoxification period or fast followed by a strict live-it eschewing salt, oils, advanced products of fermentation, excito-toxic spices such as chili peppers, excess onion, garlic,

8

strong curries and of course concentrated sweets. When reversing serious disease such as diabetes or cancer or coronary artery disease a 100% raw pattern of food consumption is needed. I recommend, to help heal your disease, you consult us or another institute of nutritional medicine and natural hygiene personally to help you build your remedial food consumption pattern individualized to your own body constitution. If you are healthy and looking for delicious meals to please your family that won't make them sick and will promote their health and well-being, look no further —this is the book.

Ama has as bonus, included the recipe for my previously secret famous chocolate shake, the recipe of which I was inspired by Cafe Gratitude in San Francisco. If you like chocolate shakes and don't like mine I will personally give you your appetite back. Enjoy!

Remember when you are making your choices for what to eat; If you can't eat it raw — just say naw.

Nana Kwaku Opare, MD, MPH, BS, CA

Author of The Rule Book and User Guide For Healthy Living

Opare Institute, Atlanta, GA

www.opare.net

Introduction

My Journey To Veganism: In 2007 Nana Kwaku Opare, MD, MPH, CA formally introduced me to veganism and the live or raw food diet. Before that time I ate the typical SAD (standard American diet) although I had been a veggie-wanna-be for decades. I had vegetarian envy. I had long felt this was the best way to eat but I didn't know how to do it. I would give it a try for a bit but it didn't last long. Somehow I could never stick to it. I didn't have support at home, and I didn't really know how to sustain it. I also didn't know how bad my diet really was. I was 50 years old and worried about my health declining as I aged. I have a family history of diabetes, cancer, high blood pressure and heart disease.

Nana Kwaku told me in very clear terms what the dangers of eating animal products are. I learned what a vegan eats and how delicious the food can be. And I learned how much better I could feel and look in a very short period of time. I made the commitment to do it this time.

I was surprised at how easy it was once I had the education and the support. And I was amazed at how good I felt and how the weight fell off within a few weeks. My skin cleared up. My headaches became less severe and less frequent. All of the health concerns I was having began to disappear or dramatically improve.

Today I can't imagine going back. I am healthier and happier than ever. I enjoy my food and have learned about so many new and delicious options.

Food For The Soul Is Born: I recognized that the work Nana Kwaku was doing with his patients fit well with my calling. As an educator I have always focused on helping people discover their best selves. I believe each of us is divinely created and has a purpose to fulfill in this lifetime. Unfortunately our current culture based on greed and profit depends on us disconnecting from this purpose and our true selves. This is especially true for us as people of Afrikan descent.

We have dedicated our work to helping our Afrikan/Black community reclaim our health, strength and discovering or re-discovering our best selves through making diet and lifestyle changes. My role in this work is once again as an educator, helping you go from being a veggie-wanna-be to becoming strong and confident as a vegan or raw vegan.

I have fed many people, helping them discover how delicious vegan and raw food is. I have shared recipes, taught classes, and answered hundreds and hundreds of questions. Over the years our patients and friends have asked me to put my recipes together in a book. With this publication I have fulfilled that request. This book as well as the information found on our Food For The Soul site (http://foodforthesoul.opare.net) is here to support you on your journey. All of the recipes in this book are vegan. Most are raw or mostly raw.

Using This Book: We like very flavorful food. Please adjust seasonings to fit your own tastes and preferences. I always suggest making a recipe more than once. The first time follow the recipe and make notations about what you liked and what you want to change the next time to make it your own. Experiment, experiment, experiment!

Food For The Soul is a community. Please come over to the site and join. Leave comments, participate in the forums, post your recipes. We are building a global nation of black vegetarians. Join The Revolution!

Acknowledgments: Above all I would like to thank the Creator and the Ancestors for all the blessings and the opportunity to do this important work. I thank my Mother and my Grandparents for teaching me to cook and to experiment when I was growing up. I thank my Father for his encouragement and my daughters Kailey and Erika for for the inspiration to be my best.

I thank my husband and partner Nana Kwaku Opare, MD, MPH, CA for teaching me, supporting me, loving me and challenging me to grow and believe in myself. My life has changed for the better in so many ways.

I thank Safi and Ade Toure my dear friends who have been doing this much longer than me for supporting our work, co-leading classes, providing recipe inspiration, copy editing and for in general being there in what ever way is needed. Medase Pa!

Thank you Vanya Francis for your friendship and sisterhood support as a fellow entrepreneur, and your review of this manuscript.

Thank you to all the patients and students at Opare Integrative Health Care and the Opare Institute for your inspiration and your willingness to learn and heal. I love watching the transformations!

Blessings to you all. See you over at Food For The Soul, The Online Home For Black Vegetarians.

Ama Opare

Equipping Your Kitchen

Eating vegan and especially raw vegan does require some kitchen re-tooling. Some items may be expensive but you don't need to get everything right away. Look for refurbished items or used items at thrift shops or on-line on sites like ebay or shopgoodwill.com.

High Speed Blender - If you can only afford one high ticket item make it a high speed blender. It makes short work of making smoothies, dressings, batters etc and for grinding nuts and seeds. The two most popular brands are Vita-Mix and Blendtec. We have the Blendtec.

Food Processor - This is a must. Fortunately, you can make do with an inexpensive one. You can often find used ones. The food processor is great for making pates, pie crusts, doughs, and for general chopping. If you have shredding and slicing blades it will make short work of prepping food for your recipes.

Juicer - There are a wide variety of types of juicers depending on what you plan to juice. For general juicing a centrifugal juicer is quick and will juice most fruits and veggies well. Either the Omega or Breville brands are quality juicers.

Citrus Juicer - There is nothing like fresh squeezed orange juice. A good citrus press makes quick work of this job. It also makes using fresh lemon or lime juice in recipes a snap. We use the manual Hamilton Beach press. You can find powered citrus juicers on the market as well.

Dehydrator - For raw foodists a dehydrator really widens the range of recipes you can use. Ditch the microwave and put your dehydrator in its place. My favorite is the Sedona Rawfood Dehydrator by Tribest.

Sharp Knives - One key part of eating healthy is preparing things yourself instead of relying on pre-chopped, pre-made food. A good set of sharp knives (and a knife sharpener to keep them that way) will make your time in the kitchen go faster and smoother.

Garlic Press - I use a LOT of garlic. Fresh garlic adds so much flavor to all types of foods. A garlic press makes mincing garlic a breeze.

Other items to have on hand are peelers, graters, measuring spoons, cutting boards, measuring cups, strainers etc. These items are inexpensive and will make your kitchen prep easier.

For more information go to http://foodforthesoul.opare. net/equipping-your-vegan- kitchen/.

Top 10 Ingredients In My Pantry

1. NAMA SHOYU
An unpasteurized soy sauce. Can be hard to find. Coconut Aminos is another raw option.

3. CHIPOTLE PEPPER POWDER
Adds a smoky spice to your dish. A great alternative to black pepper for a change of pace.

5. ITALIAN SEASONING
Fast and easy flavor for dressings, marinated veggies and sauces. This is my go to herb seasoning.

7. DULSE FLAKES
An Atlantic seaweed that adds a salty seafood flavor to dressings, pate, sauces.

9. HIMALAYAN CRYSTAL SALT
Grind this mineral rich salt in a salt grinder. Purchase on line for best price.

2. MIRIN

Sweet rice cooking wine. Adds sweetness to dressings. Use ONLY Eden brand. Other brands are mainly sugar water.

4. GARLIC

I prefer elephant garlic. It is easier to use but regular garlic is easier to find. Use either.

6. LEMONS/LIMES

Sour and tart flavor that makes your dish pop. Always use fresh squeezed.

8. MEDJOOL DATES

Soft sweetness to replace sugars. Can be soaked in water and blended to replace liquid sweetners

10. NUTRITIONAL YEAST

For cheesy, buttery flavors. Use in recipes or sprinkle on pizza, veggies, popcorn. Fortified products are a source of B-12.

The 5 Flavors

The secret to creating amazing flavor packed dishes is layering the five flavors, sweet, sour, bitter, salty and spicy.

This can be seasonings or other ingredients.

Salty: nama shoyu, coconut aminos, salt, soy sauce, sea weed, miso.

Sweet: mirin, dates, raisins, dried fruit, coconut nectar, coconut sugar, honey.

Sour: limes, lemons, oranges, vinegars, tamarind, sauerkraut.

Bitter: dark greens, citrus zest, herbs.

Spicy: dried chili peppers, fresh hot peppers, ground pepper, curry.

Layer the flavors in individual dishes or in the meal as a whole. The amounts you use will depend on your personal preferences.

The Most Important Ingredient: YOU!

Yes, there are new gadgets, appliances and ingredients that you need when transitioning to a vegan lifestyle and kitchen. However, the most important thing you need is you! Here is what I recommend to anyone learning how to incorporate vegan or raw vegan dishes into their diets.

- Experiment, Experiment, Experiment! Don't be afraid to substitute ingredients.

- As you make changes to a recipe make notes about what you did and how you liked it.

- Remember that you will learn as much by recipes that flop as you will from recipes that are winners.

Check out this YouTube video at
http://www.youtube.com/watch?v=h-56IkIjdeo

Ingredients To Watch Out For

If you are eating vegan (meaning NO animal products) you will find that animal products are often hidden in strange places. This is especially true for packaged and processed food.

ALWAYS check the labels. Even many veggie burgers or other "fake meat or dairy" products include animal products. Companies also change the ingredients from time to time. Just because it is vegan today doesn't mean it will always be vegan.

Animal Based Label Items to Avoid (often seen in packaged goods)

Casein – A milk protein that is often in items marked "non-dairy"

Ghee – Clarified butter-common in Indian food

Albumen – protein found in egg whites

Oleic acid – fat from sheep or cattle

Rennin/Rennet – enzymes from a calf's stomach

Calcium Stearate – a mineral derived from hogs and cattle

Gelatin – protein from animal bones, cartilage, tendons, and skin

Glyerides (mono/di/tri) – glycerol from animal fats

Stearic acid – animal fats and oils

Lecithin – phospholipids often from animal tissues and eggs

Pepsin – enzymes gathered from pigs stomachs

The best way to avoid these ingredients is to eat whole foods such as fresh fruits, vegetables, nuts, seeds and grains. However, I know that especially when you are new to veganism, vegan meat and dairy substitutes can be a helpful transition food while you are getting used to eating in a different way.

Fortunately there are many VEGAN alternatives. Many are even available in your local grocery store. Go to http://www.peta.org/living/vegetarian-living/our-favorite-products.aspx for PETA's list of their favorite vegan substitutes.

Breakfast and Beverages

Hearty Fruit Salad

Breakfast is often the easiest to eat raw. Smoothies are our usual breakfast but this hearty fruit salad is a great change of pace.

It is very adaptable to what ever fruit you have on hand. Choose the ripest seasonal and organic fruits you can find for optimal flavor and nutrition. Vary this recipe by using your favorite nuts or seeds.

Directions

Cut fruit into bite-sized pieces, removing skin or seeds as needed. Add to a medium sized bowl.

Add seeds and nuts. Mix well.

Serve immediately.

Other options are orange or grapefruit sections, grapes, kiwi, melons, pears, you name it! This one has endless possibilities.

Watch this video to learn how to cut a mango and a kiwi. http://www.youtube.com/watch?v=WqxlS1B4jEk

Ingredients

4 fresh figs

1 apple

1 banana

1 cup pineapple, mango, peaches or cherries

1 cup berries

¼ cup hemp seeds or chia seeds

¼ cup sunflower or pumpkin seeds or sprouted buckwheat

¼ cup nuts (optional)

How To Cut A Mango And Kiwi

Fruit Smoothie

This vitamin and energy packed breakfast is easy to make, easy to take on the road, and will get you going. Who needs coffee?

There are endless variations depending on the juice, fruit, greens, and the nuts or seeds you use. Get creative!

Fresh organic ingredients are always best but frozen will work too if fresh is not available. I put bananas that are getting too ripe in the freezer (peel them first) to use on days when my fresh supply is gone.

Don't be afraid of adding greens to your smoothie. It is a great way to get more greens into your diet. Even your kids will probably drink them this way.

Directions

Peel fruit as necessary. Cut large and/or hard fruit into smaller pieces.

Put all ingredients except ice in a high-speed blender. Put softer fruit at the bottom, harder ones at top.

Blend well. Add ice and blend again.

Serve or pour in travel bottle and take it with you.

Ingredients

2 cups fresh squeezed OJ or coconut water or apple juice

1 banana

1 cup berries

1 cup other fruit of your choice: pineapple, mango, peaches, apples, kiwi etc.

1 handful of greens: kale, lettuce, spinach, chard etc. (optional)

¼ cup chia or hemp seeds or soaked almonds, or other nuts.

2-3 cups ice

Chia Porridge

If you are used to having a hot cereal, here is a recipe for you. This is a raw alternative to oatmeal.

Chia seeds absorb liquid and become gelatinous when soaked. They have a consistency similar to tapioca. This version makes a warm porridge.

Directions

Place chia seeds in a medium sized bowl. Pour hot water into bowl. (For a raw version use hot but not boiling water.) Set aside. Stir every 5 minutes or so for 15-20 minutes.

Meanwhile, slice bananas and cut up the fruit into bite-sized pieces.

Divide fruit and nuts between two cereal sized bowls. Stir to mix.

Mix cinnamon and sweetener into the soaked chia seeds.

Add chia porridge to the fruit in the cereal bowls. Stir to mix.

Top each with ½ of the nut or seed milk and serve.

Ingredients

½ cup chia seeds

1 cup hot water

½ cup nut or seed milk

½ banana

½ cup berries or mixed cut up fruit

¼ cup pumpkin seeds (optional)

1 tsp cinnamon

1-2 TBL coconut nectar or sweetener of your choice.

Almond Milk

For years I had been saying that I had heard how easy it was to make almond milk. Somehow I just never gave it a try.

Recently I broke down and did it! Now I am making it regularly to use in hot cocoa, in chia porridge and more.

Directions

Soak almonds in water overnight or for 8 hours.

Drain and rinse the nuts. Place them and the water in a high speed blender and blend on high for 60 seconds or so, until there are no chunks of nuts.

(For a sweetened almond milk add the optional ingredients to the blender along with the nuts.)

Place a nut milk bag or cheese cloth in a large bowl. Pour milk into the bag or cloth. Squeeze the bag or cloth until you are left with just the nut pulp in the bag. Save the pulp for other recipes. (You can dehydrate or freeze it if you won't be using it right away.)

Pour milk into a jar with a tight fitting lid. Keep in refrigerator. Use within 5 days.

Ingredients

1 cup raw almonds

3 cups filtered water or young coconut water or a combination of the two

Optional:

2-4 pitted medjool dates (soak in water if they are hard)

½ to 1 whole vanilla bean, chopped (or ½-1 tsp non-alcoholic vanilla extract or vanilla powder)

¼ tsp cinnamon

Pinch of Himalayan crystal salt

Are Those Nuts Really Raw?

Many nuts are pasteurized even when they say they are raw. This is especially true of cashews and almonds, something that is often used in raw food recipes. You can find unpasteurized nuts in some health food stores and on-line.

Hot Chocolate

When I was little I used to have chocolate milk every night before I went to bed, made with Nestle's Quick. As an adult I would indulge in hot chocolate from time to time. When I went vegan I used almond milk instead of cow's milk. All was good.

When I starting eating a raw food diet I began to look for a suitable substitute. Nana Kwaku's special chocolate shake is very tasty but it doesn't quite fill that same place in my memory.

Here is a raw Hot Chocolate recipe. If you are not concerned about eating all raw you can use store-bought almond milk.

Directions

Put all ingredients except the hot water in your blender and blend until very smooth.

Fill your cups or mugs ½ full of mixture. Top off with hot water. Stir and serve.

Ingredients

1 cup almond milk

3 ½ TBL coconut butter (I like Nutivia brand Coconut Manna.)

3 ½ TBL raw cacao powder (use carob for a caffeine free version.)

½ tsp vanilla bean powder

4 pitted medjool dates.

Dash of salt

¾ cup almost boiling water

Ingredients

½ cup dehydrated sprouted buckwheat

¼ cup raw nuts

½ banana

½ cup berries or mixed cut up fruit

¼ cup pumpkin seeds

¼ cup sunflower seeds

¼ cup raisins

1 tsp cinnamon

1-2 TBL coconut nectar or sweetener of your choice (optional)

½ cup nut or seed milk

Here is a cold cereal that is raw, filling, and crunchy. For the buckwheat see the Buckwheat Crispies recipe on page 121.

Directions

Add the buckwheat, raisins, nuts and seeds to a small mixing bowl.

Slice bananas and cut up the fruit into bite-sized pieces. Add to bowl.

Add the cinnamon and sweetener and mix.

Divide cereal between to cereal bowls.

Top each with ½ of the nut or seed milk and serve.

Salads and Sides

Spicy Kale Salad

A spicy, and slightly creamy kale salad with sun-dried tomatoes and red onion. Make it even creamier by mashing the avocado into the dressing.

I find kale has a way of jumping out of the bowl when I am tossing it with the dressing. I use a VERY large bowl. You can find one at IKEA.

Directions

Dice the sun-dried tomatoes and soak in water in a small bowl and set aside.

Tear kale into bite-sized pieces and place in a very large bowl.

Slice onion very thin and add to kale.

Chop avocado and add to salad.

Mince garlic or use garlic press and add to salad.

Mix the dressing ingredients in a small bowl. Taste and adjust seasoning, adding more chipotle chili pepper powder to reach desired hotness.

Drain the sun-dried tomatoes and add to salad.

Pour dressing over salad and toss to mix well.

Ingredients

Dressing:

2 TBL Nama Shoyu

2 TBL honey

Juice of ½ lemon

3 TBL olive oil

⅓ cup nutritional yeast

1 TBL dulse flakes

1 TBL Italian seasoning

½ – 1 tsp chipotle chili powder

Salad:

1 bunch kale

½ small red onion

⅓ cup sun-dried tomatoes

1 avocado chopped

2 garlic cloves minced

Dr. O's Kale Salad

This is the kale salad Nana Kwaku first introduced me to when I was just learning about veganism and raw veganism. This is how it all started for me in learning how to create my own dressings and recipes.

He often likes to serve it with Soba noodles.

Directions

Salad:

Rinse kale and tear into bite sized pieces– you can use any variety of kale you like. We usually use green curly kale. Place in a very large bowl.

Slice and cut the avocado into bite sized pieces and add to salad.

Add the sprouts – you can use mung beans sprouts, alfalfa sprouts or whatever sprouts you prefer.

Dressing:

Mix together the dressing ingredients in a small bowl. Once you are familiar with the recipe you can just add them right to the salad.

Pour dressing over salad and toss well.

Ingredients

Salad:

1 bunch kale

1 avocado

¼-½ cup sprouts

Dressing:

3 TBL Nama Shoyu

3 TBL mirin

4 TBL sesame oil

1 TBL brown rice vinegar

2 TBL dulse flakes (a seaweed)

2 cloves of garlic

⅛ tsp chipotle chili powder

Kale and Fig Salad

Ingredients

1 bunch green kale

6-8 figs

¼ cup pine nuts

3 TBL olive oil

2 TBL balsamic vinegar

1 TBL mirin

1 TBL dulse flakes

Salt and pepper to taste (start with ½ tsp.)

I see organic figs in the market from time to time but didn't know how to use them. I decided to figure it out.

This recipe is my twist on a salad recipe I found on-line. It is super fast, easy AND delicious!

Use soft, ripe figs.

Directions

Wash and de-stem kale and tear into bite sized pieces and place in a very large bowl.

Remove stems from Figs and cut into quarters or smaller and add to kale.

Add remaining ingredients and toss to mix well. Add more pepper to taste.

Let marinate for 30 minutes before serving to soften or eat right away.

About Figs

Two common types of Figs are Black Mission Figs and Brown Turkey.

Black Mission figs are smallish, with blackish purple skin and dense pink flesh heavily studded with seeds. When ripe they are sticky and may ooze a bit of syrup.

Brown Turkey figs have a brownish dark purple skin. They are less sweet than the Black Mission and have a milder flavor.

Ripe figs are soft and may crack easily. Use them quickly.

Harvest Kale Salad

This is always a crowd pleaser. Combines Kale and Arugula with Apples or Pears in an Italian vinaigrette dressing to create a spicy and sweet salad.

There are many ways to switch this one up. Vary the greens or fruit used or the herbs in the dressing.

Directions

Wash and de-stem the kale and tear into pieces. Place in a very large bowl. Wash and drain the arugula and add to the bowl.

Core the apple or pear and cut into bite-sized pieces. Chop the celery. Add both to bowl.

Add nuts and dried cranberries to bowl and mix well.

Whisk remaining ingredients together in a small bowl. Taste and adjust seasoning as needed. Pour over salad. Toss gently.

Ingredients

1 bunch kale greens

½ bunch arugula

1 apple or ripe pear

1 stalk celery

¼ cup dried cranberries

¼ cup pecans or walnuts whole or pieces

2-3 TBL olive oil

1 lemon, juiced

¼ cup sweet mirin

Fresh or dry minced garlic to taste

2-3 TBL Nama Shoyu

1 TBL dulse flakes

¼ tsp black pepper, or chipotle pepper

¼ cup fresh or 1 TBL dried herbs of your choice

Sweet and Sour Cucumber Salad

On hot summer days this cooling salad will cool and satisfy you. Choose organic produce and leave the peels on.

Directions

Slice veggies and fruit very thin. Use a mandolin or the slicing blade on your food processor for fast, even slicing. Or use a knife. Place in a bowl.

Combine dressing ingredients in a small bowl and mix well. Pour over salad and toss to mix. Cover and refrigerate for at least 30 minutes.

Types of Cucumbers

English Cucumbers are long and thin, with dark green skin. They are often sold wrapped in plastic. It has a mild, almost non-existent flavor, thin skin and minimal seeds.

Green Cucumbers are the most common cucumbers in North America. They are relatively smooth skinned and dark green. Cucumbers sold at grocery stores tend to be waxed. Un-waxed varieties can also be found.

Lemon Cucumbers are yellow and round, the size of a generous fist and look like lemons. They are sweet, without that bitter edge of most cucumbers, and have thin skins, minimal soft seeds, and flavorful.

Ingredients

1 large or 2 small cucumbers

1 large apple

5-7 radishes

½ small sweet onion

Dressing:

3 TBL olive oil

3 TBL raw apple cider vinegar

1 TBL date or coconut sugar or date paste

1 TBL stone ground mustard

2 cloves garlic minced

1 tsp fresh ground black pepper

Brussels Sprout Slaw With Sunflower Seed Mayo

Nana Kwaku loves Brussels sprouts. This is a different twist on the usual slaw recipe. It is crunchy, flavorful, with a creamy sunflower seed dressing.

Directions

Slice Brussels sprouts very thin using the slicer blade on your food processor.

Shred carrots.

Place vegetables in a bowl.

For the sunflower mayo combine remaining ingredients in your blender and blend until smooth. Pour over the vegetables and stir well.

Ingredients

1 pound Brussels sprouts

1 large carrot

Sunflower Seed Mayo:

½ cup sunflower seeds

¼ cup olive oil

2 garlic cloves

¼ cup chopped onion

1 TBL apple cider vinegar

1 TBL Italian seasoning

1 tsp salt

1 ½ tsp ground pepper

Spinach Salad

My favorite salad at our favorite raw food restaurant is the spinach salad. I usually try to figure out what is in what I like so I can recreate it at home. This is my version of the Lovin It Live spinach salad.

On occasion I have used leftover guacamole to make this as well.

Directions

Wash spinach and add to large bowl.

Chop tomatoes, red onion and red bell pepper and add to bowl.

In a small bowl mash the avocado using a fork. You can leave some small chunks of avocado if you wish.

Add the lime juice, hot peppers, garlic and cilantro and mix well. You are basically making a somewhat thin, but not watery guacamole. Add more lime juice as needed.

For more heat add more hot peppers. Add salt to taste.

Add avocado mix to the salad and toss well or use hands to spread the mix over all the spinach.

Taste again and adjust the seasoning.

Ingredients

1 bag baby spinach

1 avocado

1 or 2 limes, juiced

½ to 1 jalapeño or serrano pepper, chopped very fine

½ cup chopped red onion

2 roma tomatoes

2 cloves garlic

½ red bell pepper

½ cup chopped cilantro

Salt to taste

Ethiopian Collard Greens

Many people think you can not eat Collard Greens raw. How wrong they are! This spicy recipe brings together the flavors of East Africa with the living food cuisine. There are a number of spices in this dish that you may not yet have in your spice rack.

Make this one ahead of time and let the greens marinate for up to a day before serving.

Directions

De-stem collard greens and stack leaves together. Roll them into a log and slice into thin strips. Place in a large mixing bowl.

Soak sun-dried tomatoes in a small bowl in water for 15-30 minutes or while you are preparing the rest of the salad.

Chop the bell pepper, onion and tomatoes and add to bowl.

Mince or chop very fine the garlic and the chili pepper. Peel and grate the ginger. Add these to the salad. Toss to mix.

Drain the soaked sun-dried tomatoes and add to bowl. Add the liquid ingredients and spices and toss well.

Let marinate for several hours or overnight to soften the collards.

*Uziza is a West African pepper. While it isn't Ethiopian it adds a distinctive flavor. You can find it at some international grocery stores.

Ingredients

1 bunch collard greens
1 red or orange bell pepper
1 red onion
2 cloves garlic
2 roma tomatoes
½ cup diced sun-dried tomatoes
1-2 green chili pepper
1-inch piece ginger
¼ cup olive oil
¼ cup Nama Shoyu
¼ cup apple cider vinegar
2 TBL coconut nectar or mirin
⅓ cup raisins
1 tsp Uziza* spice or fresh ground pepper
¼ – ½ cup nutritional yeast
½ tsp turmeric
½ tsp cardamom
⅛ tsp nutmeg
⅛ tsp fenugreek
1/16 tsp ground cloves
½ tsp cinnamon

53

Marinated Broccoli

This recipe dates way back to my childhood, long before I knew anything about "raw foods". My mom would marinate broccoli in Italian dressing. It was always a hit at pot-lucks and cook-outs.

My version uses fresh ingredients and has so many different variations. It can be given a Asian flair, a Mexican flavor, Cajun, whatever your pleasure is.

Directions

Cut veggies into bite-sized pieces. Place in large bowl or a container with a air tight lid.

Combine marinade ingredients in a small bowl and mix well.

Pour marinade over veggies and toss to distribute marinade or put lid on and shake.

You can eat it right away or to intensify the flavor and soften the vegetables let sit and stir for 30 minutes or for several hours, stirring from time to time. You can also put them in a large zip top bag, remove all the air, and then just flip the bag every so often.

Variations:

Mexican: cilantro, cumin, ground oregano, lime juice and chipotle pepper powder and marinate zucchini, peppers, and corn ;

Asian: sesame oil and add ginger and orange juice and a few drops of toasted sesame oil to marinade snow peas and/or other Asian veggies.

Caribbean: thyme, curry powder, and allspice.

Ingredients

2-4 cups firm vegetables of your choice such as:

Broccoli, carrots, cauliflower, peppers, brussels sprouts, cabbage, corn cut from the cob, okra, etc.

Marinade:

2-4 TBL cold pressed extra virgin olive oil

2-3 tsp apple cider vinegar, balsamic vinegar, lime, lemon or orange juice.

2-4 TBL mirin (Eden brand)

2-3 TBL Nama Shoyu or soy sauce

1 TBL dried herbs: Italian seasoning, herbs de Provence, or other herbs of your choice or ¼ cup fresh herbs.

Un-Roasted Vegetables

Ingredients

2 cups vegetables of your choice such as:

Broccoli, carrots, cauliflower, peppers, green beans, beets.

1 red or yellow onion

2-3 garlic cloves

2-4 TBL cold pressed extra virgin olive oil

1 TBL dried herbs: Italian seasoning, herbs de Provence, or other herbs of your choice

OR ¼ cup fresh herbs.

Salt and pepper

These veggies make a great side dish, a tasty filling for wraps, or a nice addition to a salad.

You will need a dehydrator for this recipe. Allow 4-6 hours for the dehydration process.

I like to use different color bell peppers and onions to use in wraps. Green beans and onions also make a fun snack.

Directions

Cut larger veggies and onions into strips or bite sized pieces. Place into a bowl.

Mince garlic and add to bowl.

Add olive oil and herbs and salt and pepper.

Toss to coat veggies well.

Spread in a single layer on a teflex lined dehydrator tray.

Dehydrate at 110° for 4-6 hours or until veggies have softened to your taste. They should still be crunchy.

Store in a air tight container in the fridge.

Main Dishes

Nut or Seed Paté

Patés can be made in minutes and in many variations. The basic recipe is below. Make enough to last for several days. Then you can easily put together a meal the next day or take it to work with you for lunch.

Vary your paté by using different nuts or seeds, herbs, spices, or adding vegetables. Use poultry seasoning for an un-chicken salad. Add cilantro, lime and chili powder and or cumin for a Mexican flavor. Add more dulse flakes or other seaweed for a seafood flavor.

Directions

Soak nuts or seeds in water for 4-6 hours. (You can make pate´ without soaking the nuts or seeds. Add more liquid if more moisture is needed.)

Chop onions and celery

Drain the nuts or seeds and place in the bowl of your food processor. Pulse a few times to rough chop.

Add lemon juice, garlic, dulse flakes, herbs and Nama Shoyu or soy sauce.

Process ingredients in food processor until desired consistency.

Add the onions and celery and pulse to incorporate.

See the next page for ideas of what to do with your pate.´

Ingredients

2 cups raw walnuts or sunflower seeds or other nut or seed of your choice

½ onion chopped

1 celery stalk chopped

2 cloves garlic

1 TBL lemon juice

2 TBL dulse flakes

¼ cup fresh herbs of your choice or 1 TBL dried herbs

1 TBL Nama Shoyu or soy sauce

How to Use Your Paté

Once you have your paté you can:

1. Put a scoop in a half of avocado and enjoy with a tossed salad

2. Use it as a filling for Nori Rolls. Place pate, and julienned carrots, cucumber, avocado, sprouts, and mushrooms on a sheet of nori and roll tightly. Serve with wasabi (Japanese horseradish), pickled ginger and Nama Shoyu or soy sauce.

3. Use it as a filling for Collard Wraps. De-stem a collard leaf and cut in half. Layer pate and tomatoes, cucumber, avocado, bell pepper and other vegetables and roll. Or use your favorite dehydrated wrap or a tortilla.

4. Spread on dehydrated bread or crackers.

5. Stuff bell peppers or mushrooms or spread on sliced veggies.

6. Use it as a filling for tacos.

Pasta Fresca

A raw and cooked vegan blend that you can make ahead of time. Great for taking to potlucks. There are endless ways to vary this dish by switching up the type of pasta or the veggies used or even the herbs that flavor it.

Directions

Cook pasta according to package directions. Don't let it get too mushy. A bit al dente is better for this recipe.

Drain and rinse pasta and place in a large bowl.

Cut broccoli, and zucchini into bite sized pieces. Add to the bowl.

Cut carrots into matchsticks or shred. Add to the bowl.

Thinly slice the onion. Add to the bowl

Add minced garlic and the olives.

Mix the dressing ingredients and whisk or shake to blend.

Add dressing to pasta and toss to mix. Cover and let marinate for at least 30 minutes.

Ingredients

Spaghetti noodles

½ cup broccoli florets

1 carrot

½ red bell pepper

1 small zucchini or yellow squash

½ sweet onion

¼ cup baby bella mushrooms

1 tomato

2 cloves of garlic minced

¼ cup pitted kalamata olives

Dressing

2 TBL Nama Shoyu

2 TBL mirin (Eden brand)

⅓ cup olive oil

1 TBL apple cider vinegar or juice of 1 lemon

1 TBL Italian seasoning or ¼ cup chopped fresh basil

1 tsp red pepper flakes

One Pot Pasta

This is a super fast and easy recipe. In this pasta dish you cook all the ingredients along with the pasta creating a thick rich sauce. It is very quick and satisfying.

Vary the recipe by using different types of pasta and/or different veggies or different herbs. Use dried herbs instead if you don't have fresh herbs on hand.

Directions

Slice onions thinly. Slice garlic thinly or mince. Add to a pot or deep skillet. Add dried mushrooms.

Halve cherry tomatoes or chop larger tomatoes. Cut basil into thin strips Add to pot.

Add pasta to pot.

Add olive oil, red-pepper flakes.

Add water and bring to boil. Let cook stirring frequently.

Chop remaining veggies in bite sized pieces. Add these to the pot when the pasta is half-way done to keep them from getting over cooked.

Continue cooking until pasta is al dente or reaches your desired doneness.

Total cook time about 10 minutes.

Ingredients

12 ounces linguine, spaghetti or the pasta of your choice

1 cup roma tomatoes, cherry or grape tomatoes

1 small to medium onion,

4 cloves garlic

½ tsp red-pepper flakes

2 sprigs basil

2 cups of one or more of your choice of chopped vegetables; eg. broccoli, zucchini, bell pepper

2-4 TBLS extra-virgin olive oil

2 tsp salt

¼ tsp freshly ground pepper

½ cup dried mushrooms (optional). for richer flavor to the sauce.

4 ½ cups water

Un-Stir Fried Kelp Noodles

Kelp noodles are a great addition to the raw food kitchen. Sea Tangle Noodle Company's Kelp Noodles are a fat free, gluten free, raw food noodle that is easy to use and very versatile. They are thin, spaghetti like, and don't have much flavor of their own. They are ready to use right out of the package (do rinse well). The noodles are slightly crunchy.

This recipe is inspired by Ani' Phyo's Korean "Stir-Fried" Kelp Noodles with Vegetables.

I made this for a family gathering full of carnivores and they liked it too.

Directions

Thinly slice the onion and slice mushrooms. Place the onions and mushrooms in a small bowl and toss with the Nama Shoyu until mixed well. Set aside for at least 15 to 20 minutes to marinate and soften.

Rinse the kelp noodles well. Add to a large bowl.

Shred the carrot, chop broccoli or trim peas and add to bowl.

Mince garlic and add to bowl. Add mirin, and sesame oil and mix well.

Add onions and mushrooms along with the marinade. Add spinach, and toss to mix well.

Ingredients

½ small white onion

1 cup shiitake mushrooms

1 TBL Nama Shoyu

1 carrot

1-2 garlic cloves

1 tsp mirin or honey or coconut nectar

2 TBL toasted sesame oil

1 (12-ounce) package kelp noodles

1 cup spinach

½ cup broccoli or snow peas

Chili - Yes It's Raw!

This bean free chili is will satisfy your chili desires. The barley substitutes for the meat and beans and provides a nice chewy texture.

Start sprouting the barley several days before you want to serve this so plan ahead.

Directions

Soak barley overnight then sprout for 2-3 days until short roots appear. Be sure to get sproutable barley, not pearled or processed in anyway. Rinse well and drain. You should end up with about 4 cups sprouted barley.

Place the dates and sun-dried tomatoes in a small bowl and cover with water. Set aside.

Chop the bell pepper, red onion and tomatoes. Shave corn off the ear. (If you can not find fresh organic corn use 1 cup frozen organic corn.)

Add these to a large bowl along with the barley. Add spices, honey, water, olive oil and the juice from the oranges. Stir to mix well.

Drain the sun-dried tomatoes and dates. Place them along with the garlic and yellow onion in a food processor and process into a thick paste. Add a bit of water as needed to keep it moving in the food processor.

Add this paste to the bowl with the other ingredients and stir until well mixed.

Serve with chopped avocado and cilantro. If you want it warm, put it in the dehydrator for a half hour before serving.

Ingredients

2 cups barley (not pearled)

½ tsp curry

2 TBL Nama Shoyu

1 medium bell pepper

½ small red onion

1 ear of corn

½ cup chili Powder

1 TBL Italian seasoning

½ teaspoon cayenne

1 tsp chipotle pepper powder

¼ cup honey or other sweetener

1 cup water

½ cup olive oil

2 oranges

10 medium tomatoes

4 cloves garlic

1 small yellow onion

1 cup dates

1 cup sun-dried tomatoes

Wild Rice With Blueberries, Mango and Mint

Ingredients

1 package Lunberg Organic Wild Rice

1 container organic blueberries

1 ripe mango

1 large bunch mint, the fresher the better

½ cup red bell pepper

1 avocado

2-3 TBL Nama Shoyu or soy sauce

3-4 TBL mirin (Eden Brand)

1-2 tsp chipotle chili powder (more or less to taste)

Even on a raw diet you can enjoy rice. By soaking wild rice overnight it becomes soft and puffs up. I find that Lundberg brand organic wild rice works the best.

This easy and quick dish created by Dr. Opare is very flavorful and festive looking. Serve over a bed of greens or lettuce and you have a complete meal.

Directions

Place rice in a large container and cover with 6 cups water. Loosely cover container. Let rice soak for 12-24 hours at room temperature. Drain and rinse rice. Place rice in a large bowl.

Peel mango and cut into cubes. Chop the mint and the red bell pepper. Cut avocado into cubes.

Add these to the rice along with the blueberries.

Add remaining ingredients and mix well. Taste and adjust seasoning.

Add the remaining ingredients to the rice and mix well. Adjust seasoning to taste.

Watch this YouTube Video for a fast and easy way to cut an avocado. http://www.youtube.com/watch?v=V4T1a8VyZIE

73

West Afrikan Groundnut Stew

A very flavorful and satisfying traditionally hot and spicy dish. Groundnuts are legumes. Peanuts are a groundnut and are similar to the nuts used in West Africa.

Directions

Slice or chop onion. Peel and mince or grate ginger. Rough chop the garlic. Cut sweet potatoes into chunks.

Heat the vegetable oil in a large soup pot set over medium-high heat. Sauté the onions in the oil for 3-4 minutes, stirring often. Add the ginger and garlic and sauté another 1-2 minutes, then add the sweet potatoes and stir well to combine.

Rinse and drain the lentils. Chop the tomatoes and hot peppers.

Add the lentils, vegetable broth, tomatoes, hot peppers, peanut butter, peanuts, spices and stir well to combine. Bring to a simmer, cover the pot and simmer gently for 40-50 minutes, or until the lentils and the sweet potatoes are tender.

For a creamier texture use a potato masher to mash some of the sweet potatoes and lentils.

Add salt and pepper to meet your desired taste.

Stir in kale and simmer 10 minutes.

Serve over steamed brown rice.

Ingredients

3 TBL vegetable oil

1 large yellow onion

A 3-inch piece of ginger

3-4 garlic cloves

2-3 pounds sweet potatoes

3-4 tomatoes

1-2 hot peppers

2 tsp ground cumin

1 tsp ground coriander

½ tsp ground turmeric

1 bay leaf

1 tsp cayenne

½ cup dried lentils

4-6 cups vegetable broth or water

½ cup natural peanut butter, creamy or chunky

½ cup roasted peanuts

1 bunch green kale

Salt and black pepper to taste

Thai Basil Rolls

With the exception of the wrapper this is a raw dish. We love to get these at our favorite Thai restaurant. It takes a bit of practice to get the hang of rolling but don't give up! I find that the Red Rose brand wrappers work well.

Directions

You will need a large flat dish that will hold an inch of water. It should be large enough to place a wrapper in.

Remove any hard portions of the lettuce leaves. Cut the pepper, cucumber, onions into long, thin strips.

Fill the dish with hot (not boiling) water. Start by submerging one wrapper into the water. It should soften after 10-15 seconds.

Remove the wrapper from the water and place on a clean wet surface.

Layer ingredients starting with lettuce leaves toward the bottom of the wrapper. Spread out the ingredients horizontally.

Fold the sides of the wrapper over the ingredients, then bring up the bottom. Tuck the bottom around the ingredients and roll to the top of the wrapper.

Cut roll in half or into quarters.

Serve on a platter along with the Tamarind Dip Sauce.

Ingredients

5 round rice wrappers (dried)

5-10 leaf lettuce leaves

1 cups bean sprouts

½ cup fresh Thai basil or sweet basil

½ cup cilantro

¼ cup shredded carrot

½ cup red bell pepper

½ cup cucumber

3-4 spring onions,

½ package Enoki mushrooms

Enoki Mushrooms

Tamarind Dip Sauce

A sweet, spicy and tangy sauce that goes great with Thai Basil Rolls.

Tamarind is the pod of the tamarind tree. The pods are full of seeds, fibrous strands, and pulp.

You can find whole dried tamarind in international grocers. You can also find blocks of the pulp with the seeds and fibers. The easiest to use is the tamarind paste that comes in a jar and has the seeds and fibers removed.

Directions

Place tamarind paste in a small bowl. If you are using the paste block, soak ¼ of the paste in hot water to soften. Press through strainer to remove any seeds or pulp.

Chop chilies very fine. Add to bowl.

Add remaining dipping sauce ingredients together (except peanuts).

Mix well. Pour into small low dishes. Top with chopped peanuts.

Ingredients

2 TBL tamarind paste

1-2 TBL coconut nectar

1 TBL Nama Shoyu

1 clove garlic

1 green or red chili OR ½ tsp. dried crushed chili or cayenne pepper

¼ cup chopped peanuts

Pizza

Raw pizza is a great recipe to make a quick dinner if you have the components made ahead of time. The crust keeps well in an air tight container in the fridge. The sauce and cheeze can be stored for a week. Then all you have to do on a busy day is chop the toppings and throw it together.

Plan ahead and make the crust and the Sage Crumbles a day or two before you want to serve pizza.

Directions

Chop the avocado, bell pepper, onion and mushrooms into bite sized pieces.

Place onions and mushrooms in a small bowl. Add olive oil and nama shoyu and stir to coat evenly. Set aside to marinate for 10 minutes

Spread cheeze evenly over pizza crust.

Spread marinara sauce over cheeze.

Evenly distribute remaining ingredients over pizza.

Use a pizza cutter to cut into slices.

Ingredients

Pizza Crust

Sage Crumbles

1 cup Marinara Sauce

1 cup Cheeze

1 avocado

½ red bell pepper

½ small onion

½ cup black olives

6 button or baby bella mushrooms

1 cup sprouts

2 TBL olive oil

1 TBL Nama Shoyu or Soy Sauce

½-1 tsp red pepper flakes (optional)

Pizza Crust

Making this crust is super easy. You will need a dehydrator. It calls for sprouted and dehydrated buckwheat but you can just use raw buckwheat in a pinch. I usually make up a bunch of sprouted buckwheat and keep it in a jar in my fridge so it is ready when I need it.

Directions

Grind Buckwheat and flax seeds into a powder in your high speed blender, set aside.

Place the celery, carrots, olive oil, salt, and water in a high-speed blender. Blend until smooth. Add the flax meal and buckwheat powder and blend to mix well.

Scoop the batter onto a lined dehydrator tray. Spread the batter evenly across the entire surface.

Dehydrate for 10 hours at 104F. Flip and score into your desired shape, either a circular pie or 9 slices. Dehydrate for another 4 to 6 hours, until the crust has your desired consistency.

If you let it get very dry it will store in the refrigerator for several weeks in an air tight container. You are then ready to make a fast meal. I usually cut it into serving sized pieces before storing.

Ingredients

½ cup sprouted and dehydrated buckwheat

2 cups chopped celery

1 cup chopped carrots

2 TBL olive oil

½ tsp sea salt

1 cup water

¾ cup flax seed

Sage Burgers and Sausage Crumbles

This easy recipe makes wonderful burger patties, tasty crumbles for pizza and other dishes, or could be formed into a loaf.

Directions

Chop onion. Peel and core apple. Place in food processor bowl along with other ingredients.

Blend in food processor until well blended.

Sage Burger:

Form into patties 1/2 inch thick and place on mesh dehydrator sheet. Dehydrate at 110° for 4-6 hours, until firm and moist but not soggy on the inside.

Sausage Crumbles:

Drop 1 teaspoon full of mixture on teflex sheet. You want this to resemble crumbled sausage. Dehydrate at 110° for 2-4 hours, until firm and moist but not soggy on the inside.

Meatloaf:

Form into a loaf 2 inches thick. Dehydrate at 110° for 6-8 hours, until firm and moist but not soggy on the inside.

Ingredients

2 cups pecans

1 small white onion

1 small sweet apple

1 cup mushrooms (any type)

1/3 cup olive oil

1 tsp fennel seeds (ground)

2 tsp sea salt

1 1/2 tsp black pepper

2 TBL sage (rubbed)

2 tsp thyme

Sauces & Dressings

Marínara Sauce

Marinara sauce has many uses. This recipe makes enough to use several times. Store it in an air tight container in your refrigerator for 5 days.

Use it as a pizza sauce, sauce on your spiralized veggies, in raw lasagna, a topping for burgers, on kelp noodles, or as the base for a salad dressing.

Directions

Put sun-dried tomatoes and dates in a bowl and cover with water. Set aside for at least 30 minutes.

Chop tomatoes and place in your food processor.

Drain sun-dried tomatoes and dates and add to food processor.

Add remaining ingredients to a food processor and process until smooth.

Ingredients

2 ½ cups roma tomatoes

½ cup sun-dried tomatoes,

3 organic dates, pitted

¼ cup olive oil

4 cloves garlic

2 tsp Italian seasoning

½ cup loosely packed basil

1 tsp sea salt

⅛ tsp cayenne

⅛ tsp red pepper flakes

Raw Nut or Seed Cheeze

Raw Cheezes are used for pizza, to fill collard wraps, to spread on breads and crackers, as a dip, and more.

Try using a variety of seeds and nuts until you find the taste you like. Add fresh herbs, or peppers for even more variety.

Directions

Place all ingredients in your high speed blender.

Blend until creamy. Add more water if needed to reach your desired consistency.

Store in an air-tight container in your refrigerator for up to a week.

Ingredients

1 cup cashew or macadamia nuts or a combination

1 TBL lemon juice

1 TBL Nama Shoyu or Coconut Aminos

¼ cup water

Variations:

Replace nuts with Sunflower seeds or Pumpkin Seeds

Add ½ to 1 red bell pepper (reduce or eliminate water as needed to reach desired consistency.)

Salsa

Salsa is one of those raw foods that most folks have been eating for years. Freshly made salsa adds a spicy kick to many dishes. Add to wraps, top pate´, dip your chips etc.

Directions

Chop tomatoes or pulse briefly in food processor. You want smallish chunks but not mush.

Chop onion very fine. Mince garlic.

Mince jalapeño pepper. For milder salsa de-seed pepper before chopping.

Chop cilantro.

Optional: shred carrot.

Place chopped ingredients in a medium bowl.

Add lime juice and mix well. Add salt to taste.

Ingredients

3 roma tomatoes

1 small red onion

2-3 garlic cloves

½ bunch cilantro

Juice of 1-2 limes

1 jalapeño pepper

½ carrot (optional)

Salt to taste

Guacamole

Guacamole could easily be classified as a side dish or a salad as well. Serve it with chips, use it to fill tacos or burritos, fill a collard green wrap, or as a dip for raw veggies.

Directions

Mash the avocado in a medium bowl.

Chop tomatoes or pulse briefly in food processor. You want smallish chunks but not mush. Add to the avocado.

Chop onion very fine. Mince garlic.

Mince jalapeño pepper. For milder guacamole seed pepper before chopping.

Chop cilantro.

Add chopped ingredients to the bowl and mix well.

Add lime juice and cumin and mix well. Add salt to taste.

Ingredients

3 very ripe avocados

2 roma tomatoes

1 small red onion

2-3 garlic cloves

½ bunch cilantro

Juice of 1-2 limes

½ tsp cumin

1-2 jalapeño peppers

salt to taste

Vinaigrette

Homemade salad dressings tastes so much better than bottled dressings. Once you learn how to make your own you won't want to use the bottled ones anymore. Watch this video for more. http://www.youtube.com/watch?v=Iv1t9-aM5A4

Vinaigrette dressings are a key part of a vegan and raw food kitchen. They can also be used as a marinade as well as a base for a sauce.

There are many variations that you can make just by using different oils, different vinegar, different spices and different seasonings to create flavors from around the world.

Directions

Place ingredients in a jar with a lid, shake well and dress your salad.

Variations:

For balsamic vinaigrette use balsamic vinegar.

For Asian flavor use sesame oil and a few drops of toasted sesame oil.

For citrus dressing replace the vinegar with lemon juice or lime juice.

Replace Italian seasoning with fresh herbs.

Watch the International Spices and Seasoning video for more ideas of customizing your dressing.
http://www.youtube.com/watch?v=A9323_dPySI

Ingredients

3 TBL olive oil

1 TBL apple cider vinegar

1 TBL Nama Shoyu or Soy Sauce

1 TBL mirin

½ TBL Italian seasoning

1 tsp ground pepper

Desserts

Brownies

I remember how hard it was to wait to eat freshly made baked brownies. It took long to make, bake, and then you had to wait until they cooled enough to slice.

This is a super easy recipe that you can make and be ready to eat in 15 minutes. Make a double batch! You wont' be sorry. :-)

Top with raw chocolate cream for an even more decadent dessert.

Directions

Chop ¼ cup of the walnuts and set aside.

Place the remaining walnuts and salt in a food processor and process until finely ground. Add the dates and process until mixture sticks together. Add the cocoa powder and optional vanilla and process until evenly distributed. Add the water, if using, and process briefly.

Stir in the reserved chopped walnuts. Pack the mixture firmly into a square container. Brownies will keep for up to one week in the refrigerator or one month in the freezer. (Or until your family devours them which ever comes first!)

Ingredients

1 ½ cups raw walnuts, unsoaked

Dash salt

10 pitted medjool dates, unsoaked

⅓ cup raw cacao or carob powder

½ tsp vanilla extract

2 tsp water (for a moister brownie, optional)

Chocolate Frosting/Sauce

Keep any leftover frosting in the refrigerator for several weeks for spur of the moment use.

I love to take a medjool date, put a pecan in where the pit used to be and dip in Chocolate Sauce. A raw turtle candy!

Directions

Pit dates and soak in enough water to cover for at least 15 minutes.

Melt coconut oil by setting container in hot water.

Drain dates and add to a high speed blender. Add coconut oil, cacao powder, and salt.

Blend until very smooth. Add more water if needed to keep mixture moving.

For frosting you want the finished product to be pretty thick. For a sauce add a bit more water.

This will thicken up when cold and will harden in the freezer.

Ingredients

1 cup medjool dates

Water

¼ cup raw cacao powder

¼ cup coconut oil

pinch of salt

Upside Down Cake

The cake offers many delicious variations. Use a mixture of fruit or all one type of fruit. Try mango, strawberries, blueberries, raspberries, pineapple, kiwi, bananas or apples. Use your imagination!

Directions

Mix fruit and sweetener in a bowl and set aside. Let sit at least 5 minutes.

Place coconut, walnuts and salt in the food processor and process until finely ground. Add the dates and process until the mixture begins to stick together. Do not over process. If your dates are on the hard side you may need to add a tablespoon or two of water.

Line a pie pan or cake pan with parchment paper or plastic wrap.

Place half the fruit in the pan. Spread half of the crust/cake evenly over the fruit. Press down with your hands to compress. Top with the remaining fruit and then the remaining crust/cake. Press down firmly again.

Chill the cake for half hour or longer.

To serve run a knife around the edge of pan. Place a plate upside down on the pan. Flip the plate and pan over. Tap the bottom of the pan to make sure cake loosens. Lift the pan off. Remove the parchment paper or plastic wrap.

Ingredients

2 ½ cups mixed soft fresh fruit: Berries, pineapple, mango, kiwi etc. in any combination

1 TBL date or coconut sugar or coconut nectar

1 cup shredded unsweetened coconut

1 cup raw walnuts, almonds or pecans

¼ tsp salt

6 pitted medjool dates

Key Lime Pie

On a trip to Key West I thought I should have some Key Lime Pie but we couldn't find vegan Key Lime Pie anywhere. I decided to try and make my own raw version.

Key limes are very small and you will need as many as a dozen or more. You can use regular limes as well. Don't use bottled juice!

Please don't let the avocado scare you. It adds the creamy texture, the green color, but doesn't add avocado flavor.

Directions

Grind nuts and salt in a food processor until roughly chopped. Add the dates and process until the dough sticks together well, don't over process. If your dates are a bit dry add a tablespoon of water to help mixture stick together.

Press crust into a pie pan or tart pan.

Place all the filling ingredients in your blender until smooth and creamy. Taste and adjust sweetness to your liking if needed.

Spread filling evenly over the crust. Garnish with shredded coconut or lime slices if you want to get fancy. Let it chill in the fridge for several hours, until firm.

Filling may by used to make popsicles, ice cream or eat as a pudding as well.

Ingredients

Crust:

1 cup raw, unsalted walnuts

½ cup coconut flakes

4-5 dates

Pinch of salt

Filling:

2 avocado

½ cup key lime juice (or regular lime juice)

6 TBL coconut or coconut nectar

6 TBL melted coconut oil

Pinch of salt

Pecan Pie

A rich and satisfying version of a family favorite for many folks. Take this to your next holiday dinner and you won't feel deprived.

Directions

Soak cashews in filtered water for 6 hours.

Oil the insides of pie pan or tart pan with the oil.

Pit the dates. Soak 10 of the dates in filtered water and set aside.

Place walnuts, coconut, salt and cinnamon in a food processor and process until crumbly.

Add the un-soaked dates and ground flax seeds and process until the mixture begins to stick together.

Press firmly into the bottom and sides of the pan.

Drain the soaked dates reserving the soak water. Drain and rinse the cashews.

Place the dates, cashews, lime juice, vanilla extract, coconut oil, and sea salt in the food processor and process until smooth, scraping down the sides often. If it is too dry, add 1 tablespoon of the reserved date water but only if needed.

Spread the filling over the crust.

Top with pecan halves and the chopped pecans.

Refrigerate for several hours before serving.

Ingredients

Olive oil or coconut oil to grease pie pan

1 cup raw walnuts

¼ cup shredded, unsweetened coconut

⅛ tsp salt

¼ tsp ground cinnamon

14 large Medjool dates

3 TBL ground flax seeds

Some reserved date soak water

⅓ cup raw cashews

2 tsp fresh lime juice

½ tsp vanilla extract

1 tsp unrefined virgin coconut oil, softened

⅛ tsp sea salt

20-25 raw pecan halves

½ cup chopped pecans

Nana Kwaku's Guaranteed Chocolate Shake

For the first time we are sharing the recipe for this often requested treat. In the past you had to be around when Nana Kwaku was making a shake and take down the recipe yourself.

The ingredients come from all over the world. Watch the video below to see how to open the coconut.

Be careful how late in the day you drink your shake. The cacao nibs contain caffeine and you may well find you can't sleep!

Directions

Open coconuts and pour the water into a large high-speed blender carafe. Remove the meat and place that in the blender as well. This will not work in a regular blender

Remove the pits from the dates. Add the dates and the remaining ingredients to the blender.

Blend until very smooth. This will take one and a half minutes.

Add ice. Blend again for 45 seconds.

Serve and enjoy!

Nana Kwaku says the guarantee is void if you substitute any ingredient. It just won't taste as good.

Ingredients

2 young coconuts

⅓ cup raw pecans

½ vanillia bean

3 TBL cocao nibs

9 medjool dates

1 TBL macca powder

dash or two of Hymilaian crystal salt

4 cups ice

How to open a young coconut http://www.youtube.com/watch?v=PXZsxSnUdcM

Snacks & Extras

Ants On A Log

This is a fun snack for kids and adults alike. I used to serve it when I ran a day care when my daughters were little.

It can be made raw or partially raw depending on if you have raw nut or seed butter on hand. Use dried cranberries or cherries for red ants on a log.

Directions

Cut celery sticks into desired length. I usually go for 2 inch pieces.

Spread nut or seed butter on to the celery to fill the stalk. This is your log.

Top with raisins or other dried fruit (the ants).

Enjoy!

How easy is that!!! It travels well too in a air tight container. Good for lunch boxes and snacks on the go.

Ingredients

4 celery stalks

Nut or seed butter such as:

> peanut butter
>
> almond butter
>
> tahini
>
> cashew butter

Raisins, dried cranberries or dried cherries

Kale Chips

Kale Chips are very easy to make and help satisfy that desire for a crunchy snack. Making them yourself is MUCH less expensive than buying them in the store.

Theoretically these will last for several weeks in an airtight container. Practically speaking, I find they get eaten up very fast. :-)

Directions

Wash kale and de-stem. Tear into chip sized pieces. Place in a very large bowl.

Mix remaining ingredients and pour over kale. Toss and/or massage with your hands to distribute well.

Spread kale out on mesh dehydrator trays. Don't pack them too close together. You will likely need to use 2-3 trays.

Dehydrate at 111 degrees for 24 hours or more, or until crunchy.

Store in an air tight container.

Ingredients

2 bunches of organic green kale

¼ cup olive oil

2 TBL Nama Shoyu

1 TBL mirin or honey

2 TBL nutritional yeast

1 tsp chipotle pepper powder or more for more spice.

2 tsp garlic powder

optional additions – add one or more of the following:

1 TBL curry powder

1 TBL chili powder

1 TBL cajun spice

2 tsp onion powder

Nacho Cheeze Kale Chips

These delicious raw vegan Nacho Cheeze kale chips will be gone before you know it!

Next time you are shopping get a few extra bunches of kale and make chips. They are great for snacks as well as great to pack in your lunch. They also make a nice accompaniment to your meal. They can be made as spicy as you like.

Directions

Soak cashews in water for at least an hour.

Wash and de-stem kale. Tear into chip-sized pieces. Place your kale in a very large bowl.

De-seed the bell pepper and jalapeño pepper.

Place peppers and remaining ingredients in your high-speed blender and blend until very smooth. Add more water as needed to reach a creamy pour-able consistency. You don't want it watery but you want to be able to coat the kale.

Pour the nacho cheese sauce over the kale and toss or massage with hands until every leaf is well coated.

Spread kale on dehydrator mesh sheets and dehydrate at 115° for 24 hours or until very dry and crispy.

Store your Nacho Cheeze Kale Chips in an airtight container or in zip top bags.

Ingredients

2-4 bunches of kale washed, de-stemmed and torn into chip-size pieces.

1 cup raw cashews

2 TBL nutritional yeast.

One red bell pepper

One jalapeño pepper seeded (or leave seeds for more heat).

1 tsp Himalayan crystal salt

1 tsp chipotle pepper powder. Add more for more heat

1 tsp onion powder

1 TBL mirin or sweetener of your choice.

½-1 cup water as needed to reach creamy pour-able consistency.

Sprouted Buckwheat

Raw sprouted buckwheat is great to have on hand. Make a large batch and store it in your refrigerator to use in recipes or as a cereal or to add to fruit salads.

Buckwheat is not wheat so it is a gluten free ingredient.

Directions

Wash the buckwheat thoroughly and soak overnight, preferably in filtered water. I use a large gallon size sprouting jar. You can also use a glass or Pyrex bowl covered with a clean cloth or paper towel. The water will get very thick and gelatinous like.

In the morning rinse the buckwheat and drain. Turn sprouting jar on its side or recover bowl and let sit. Repeat again at night.

In the morning your buckwheat should have short tails growing. Spread buckwheat on sheets in the dehydrator and dehydrate for 8-12 hours at 110 degrees or until fully dry.

Cool and store in an airtight container in refrigerator.

Ingredients

2 - 4 cups raw buckwheat

Spiced Nuts

Make these tasty nuts with whatever nuts you like. Try different spice combinations to suit your tastes or the theme of your meal.

Spiced Nuts make great snacks, garnishes for salads, or additions to your un-stir fries or cooked stir fry recipes.

Directions

Place nuts in a medium bowl. Add Nama Shoyu and enough water to cover nuts by ½ inch. Cover and soak for 4-8 hours or over night.

Drain nuts and rinse briefly. Place them in a mixing bowl.

Add the spices and toss to coat all nuts evenly.

For raw nuts, spread evenly on dehydrator tray and dehydrate for 24 hours or until very dry and crunchy.

Otherwise, spread evenly on baking sheet and place in oven at lowest setting until very dry and crunchy. May take several hours.

Store nuts in an airtight container in the refrigerator.

Ingredients

2 cups of raw nuts – almonds, cashews, walnuts, pecans etc.

2 TBL Nama Shoyu (or soy sauce)

water

1-2 TBL chili powder

1 tsp salt

1 tsp curry powder

1 tsp garlic or onion powder

Ama Opare, a gourmet raw vegan chef, is a lifelong educator and an experienced program director. She earned a BS in Education at Central Michigan University, a MS in Early Childhood Education and an MS in Educational Leadership at Eastern Michigan University.

Ama has provided educational opportunities for children, youth and adults in a broad range of areas since 1983. She has directed programs, developed curriculum, and taught classes for all ages. She is a published author, and public speaker.

Ama is the creator of Food For the Soul: The On-line Home For Black Vegetarians. She is an educator and revolutionary who has teamed up with her physician husband, Nana Kwaku Opare, MD, MPH, CA, to address the growing health problems in the Afrikan/Black community by building a Nation of Black Vegetarians and Vegans.

Ama says "I have spent my life helping others learn to listen to their inner-selves, to trust themselves, and to move towards becoming their best selves. I now realize that eating healthy food is an important part of being at our best. My soulful recipes combine healthy food with great taste.

I used to tell my daughters as they went off to school 'Let your light shine and you can do anything!' I look forward to helping you shine your light bright out into the world."

Food For The Soul: The On-Line Home For Black Vegetarians is located at http://foodforthesoul.opare.net. It offers a blog, recipes, e-books and on-line training for new vegetarians and for juice fasting, and a free member only forum area.

28314631R10073

Made in the USA
Charleston, SC
09 April 2014